Big Black Bears

Greg Roza

The Rosen Publishing Group, Inc.
New York

Black bears live in the forest.

Black bears like to eat fish.

Black bears sleep all winter in a cave or den.

Black bears use their short claws to climb trees.

Baby bears are called cubs.

A mother bear keeps her cubs safe.

bear

claws

cubs

den